KEN PYNE

Silly Mid On

HOW TO SURVIVE THE CRICKET SEASON

CENTURY PUBLISHING

LONDON

First published in Great Britain in 1985
by Century Publishing Co. Ltd,
Portland House,
12–13 Greek Street, London W1V 5LE

ISBN 0 7126 0784 6 (cased)
ISBN 0 7126 0735 8 (paper)

Printed in Great Britain in 1985 by
Richard Clay (The Chaucer Press) Ltd, Bungay, Suffolk

Cricket, the game of gentlemen . . .

*So nice to meet you again! It must be at least twenty
minutes since we last passed each other!*

It's a family tradition—the eldest son has used the same bat since 1748.

and is enjoyed by people all over the world . . .

Walgoola Base to Flying Doctor! . . . Walgoola Base to Flying Doctor! . . . Emergency! . . . Would you come and take over as umpire? Over.

We've come to civilize you.

But although the sun has set on the empire . . .

I think the greatest achievement of my life was turning the King of Basutoland into a damned good slow leg-spinner.

the game has been left behind and shines as brightly as ever . . .

Well, what the hell else is there to do on St. Helena?

and the young play the game today with as much enthusiasm as did our ancestors.

I got it off our mantlepiece—we can play for my granaad's ashes!

For what beach scene is complete without a game of cricket?

For heaven's sake let your father get a few runs or he'll sulk for the rest of the day.

From Grandad . . .

Just who does he think he is?

Oh, for heaven's sake let him field at square cover point!

they all enjoy the summer game . . .

Why do I always get to be deep third man?

in the same manner as the greatest of professionals.

Cricket is renowned for its sportsmanship . . .

I've just come in to tell you lads that as far as my team are concerned all that's important is that it's a good game.

and this is found at all levels.

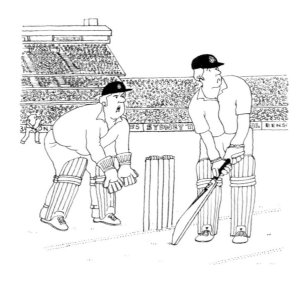

I hate to be the one to tell you but I think you ought to know—your wife is having an affair with your agent.

But it does not blunt players' keenness for the game . . .

Oh dear, he's off form today—he was aiming at your head.

or their healthy competitiveness . . .

It's the 100th batsman he's knocked out in first class
cricket.

—especially on the village green.

It's the annual village match.

Much depends, as always, on the weather . . .

Actually, we've yet to play a match.

—and on the public.

Well, it's your own fault for playing on the common.

The annual match is often the social event of the year . . .

May God forgive you!

His Lordship has bowled every year for the village since 1908.

Being the Lord of the Manor entitles him to be opening bat.

But some take it more seriously . . .

That's the last time you'll get served after hours in my pub.

than is good for them.

I'm afraid he wasn't the village idiot before we started putting him at silly point.

Good cricket . . .

Awfully sorry but we've never been a terribly good batting side so we've had to rely on tactical fielding.

deserves good ale.

He tried for years to get into the team but he was such an atrocious player—then he got a job in a brewery.

It can be found at the beginning of play,

Apparently he's confident of having a long innings.

I'm fielding in the deep.

and at the end of play.

They beat us by 36 runs but we beat them by 153 beers.

Cricket can be found in towns too,

THE GAME
EXPLAINED
TO
FOREIGNERS

but players' enthusiasm for the game is not always shared by local residents . . .

We bought it in January and couldn't understand why it was so cheap.

or others who want to enjoy the park.

It can also have disadvantages for the players,

as it can sometimes get rather crowded . . .

*Have you noticed how rapidly the spirit of cricket
evaporates on a double-booked pitch?*

—with animals as well as people.

He's pinched our bloody ball again!

Taken more seriously is club cricket . . .

As this is your first game for us, James, I'd like you to know that here we do not regard cricket as a religion—we consider it to be far more important than that.

which is sometimes all that the players live for.

My wife complained that I took cricket too seriously—so I divorced her.

Reluctant wives and girlfriends . . .

*When the vicar said 'For better or for worse', I didn't know
the 'worse' meant cricket.*

It's not that we can't afford holidays—it's just that they always clash with the cricket season!

He'd never have got into the team if it weren't for his wife's tea spreads.

They sometimes take the game so seriously . . .

Gregory looks at it this way—God must have been a cricket fan otherwise he wouldn't have created Australia.

that they eventually ruin their home life . . .

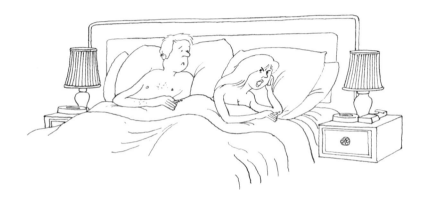

*Must you keep shouting 'Owzat!' every time we finish
making love?*

for the great god Cricket.

Cricket can also be important in business,

Most ambitious men bring their boss home for a meal—
he brings his home for net practice.

Most managerial staff, Harman, play golf *in the office!*

it can prove a great help to the rising young executive . . .

I got my promotion purely on merit—I got 120 against ICI.

—or the instrument of doom.

I had a company Jaguar XJ6, £35,000 a year and my own oak-panelled Wilton-carpeted office with a computer— then I trod on the wicket for a duck against ICI.

Cricket is a great leveller.

*We're not in the office now and here you are the captain,
so not so much of the 'sir'—I'll call you Peter and you can
call me Mr. Hargreaves.*

The most junior of clerks may be the best of bowlers,

It's being bowled by someone in a lower income bracket that I find so infuriating.

while the Chairman of the Board proves inept in the slips . . .

Oh bad luck, sir!

and the Chief Accountant incapable of mastering the complexities of the scoreboard.

Crossley! Leave my wife alone and put my last four runs up!

Although the happy works cricket team makes for a happy business . . .

We'd love to give you the job, Mr. Dawson, but I'm afraid we're looking for a slow left-hand bowler.

the game builds a comradeship that goes beyond the boundary of the office.

Look on the bright side—the company may have gone bust but at least we've stayed together as a team.

Cricket can get into the blood early . . .

We've got him down for Eton, Cambridge and the M.C.C.

—sometimes very early.

He said his first word today—it was 'googly'.

At school the best cricketer is the hero of the summer term . . .

Nobody's going to expel me—I average over a century an innings!

and the exploits of the football hero of winter are forgotten.

It always takes Moorcroft time to adjust to the change-over.

One of the advantages the game brings to city children is that it gives them the opportunity to visit the countryside . . .

I don't understand it—where are all the 'No Ball Games' signs?

and enjoy some fresh air.

For the very best player,

There's something I've got to tell you, son—you're never going to be captain of the West Indies.

a great career may lie ahead . . .

*I'm sorry, mother and father, but if you want to talk to me
you'll have to talk to my agent first.*

The lad's got an awful lot to learn about the first-class game!

I told you his bouncers were legendary.

and in front of big crowds.

It's people like me that pay your wages!

And if he can survive the pressures,

I'm terribly worried about him—every time he sees a batsman on TV he bowls him.

resist the temptations . . .

*He's got a problem—his night club scoring average is
higher than his batting average.*

**and prove he has that little bit more dedi-
cation than the other players,**

He spends four hours a day practising his appeals.

he may experience the pride of playing for his country . . .

The selectors said they saw in me the four attributes needed to make the modern test match player—aggressive bowling, sharp fielding, steady reliable batting and not banned for having played in South Africa.

and the financial rewards that go with it.

Wear a helmet? Heavens no! I'd miss out on the male modelling commissions!

He will travel the world,

It's a great life—playing for England I get to lose games all over the world!

What a hero! one more six and he's in the record book.

and scrutinized by commentators.

*That's the first time, Denis, that a cricket commentator
has drunk a bottle of scotch in one over since Barry Akers
did it in Melbourne in 1948.*

If he always remembers that above all he is a professional cricketer,

I just have to tell you that I thought your breakfast cereal TV commercial was the greatest individual performance I've ever seen by a batsman.

trains constantly,

*He's the only batsman I know who insists on having a
mid-on in the nets with him!*

keeps fit and is lucky with injuries,

*Talk about in love with the game! Instead of a box he uses
a Wisden's Cricketers' Almanack.*

then with determination and good performances . . .

You have to admire his consistency and adaptability—no matter what the wicket, he can always be relied upon to drive the crowd away.

Look, I know you're the skipper but don't you think he's bowled his fair share of overs?

Everything, sir, is your fault!

No matter what heights a cricketer reaches he must always have respect for the umpire,

Quick! Run back to the pavilion and find out what that signal means!

whose calming and distinguished presence . . .

My God! He's gone!

can determine a match whether it be on a village green, in a park or at Lords.

You're appealing against the light? Who do you think I am? God?

We mustn't forget that a cricket match would not have its unique atmosphere if it weren't for the spectators . . .

Would you please stop talking—I can't hear the commentators.

—whether it be the friendly banter between rival fans at a test match,

Sorry to wake you up, dear, but what does 'honky' mean?

running on at the end of play in celebration . . .

One of them swiped my box as a souvenir!

or even running on during it.

I wouldn't mind but he's my analyst.

These days they may be watching a women's cricket match . . .

Stop! My elastic's gone.

—as women's cricket is growing in popularity . . .

I tell you, I haven't had a single Sunday roast since she took up this bloody game.

which is as it should be,

It's easy—I just tell my husband I've got net practice!

for cricket is a game for everybody . . .

*A third-rate ventriloquist he may be but he's still the best
fast bowler we've got.*

—**whether they be young and keen,**

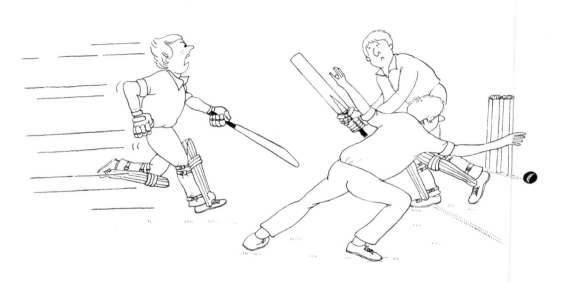

Run!

middle-aged and keen,

*Actually, I've a serious heart condition but I'm determined
to get at least one century before it kills me.*

or the ever-willing pensioner.

You're the last man in and we need 122 to win—so it all depends on you!

The game is there to be enjoyed by the commanding batsman,

*Stay! I want to give my new girlfriend the impression that
I'm in command and know what I'm doing.*

the resolute bowler,

*In all my years I've never known a bowler put such a shine
on the ball as he does.*

the wicket keeper with the razor-sharp
reflexes,

Hold it! He hasn't bowled the ball yet!

the fearless fielder,

the all-rounder,

*I know he's our best batsman and our best bowler but
now he's just showing off.*

cautious players . . .

Not for nothing has he the reputation as the most timid batsman in all New Zealand.

and aggressive ones.

*No, he doesn't play because he loves the intrinsic beauty
of the game—he just likes trying to kill people.*

For everyone from the long-suffering umpire . . .

I'm terribly sorry, but this is my last match and I've been wanting to do that for the past twenty-five years.

to the loyal and appreciative crowd,

I think you'd better wake up, sir—the match finished three hours ago.

cricket is a game of pleasure.

*Gerald says that playing cricket comes to him as easily
and naturally as making love—and I'm afraid he's right.*

It can keep you fit,

Walking to the wicket and straight back again is the only exercise he gets.

give you an excuse to spend a civilized day in the most pleasant of surroundings,

I sometimes wonder about Gordon's commitment.

and provide you with the chance to meet new people.

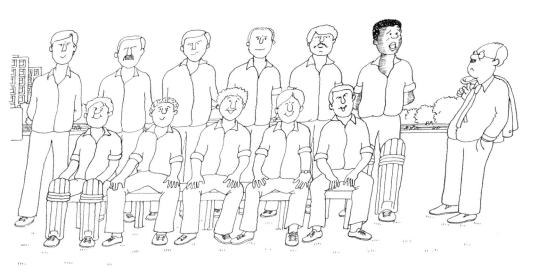

I'm the token good player.

It will never leave you short for a topic of conversation,

. . . I lifted the next one over extra cover, then leaned back in my crease and reached forty with a choice cut—by the time I'd got to fifty I'd hit eight boundaries! To celebrate my half century I moved away to leg and hit six over long-off, the next ball came off my pad—they appealed for a catch but the umpire quite rightly . . .

and it makes you a member of the most decent of sporting societies.

He's just killed a mole trying to flatten a bump on the wicket.

So there we are—recognized as one of the world's great sports,

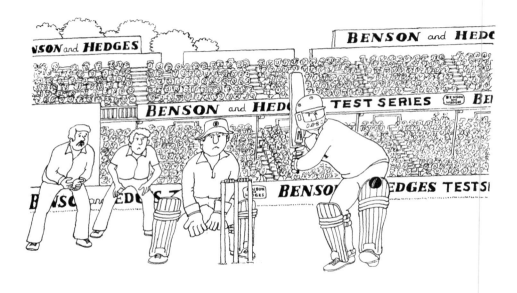

*He's one of the world's great players—he averages a
century a sponsor.*

cricket can be enjoyed all your life . . .

I've never told him that I know he's never really loved me—his heart has always belonged to the sound of leather on willow on a sunny summer's day.

—from the beginning to the end of your day's play.